**SCHOLASTIC**

# Fractured Fairy Tales Math

by Dan Greenberg

New York ❖ Toronto ❖ London ❖ Auckland ❖ Sydney
Mexico City ❖ New Delhi ❖ Hong Kong ❖ Buenos Aires

**Teaching Resources**

Cover design by Maria Lilja
Cover illustration by Doug Jones
Interior design by Kelli Thompson
Interior illustrations by Mike Moran

ISBN 0-439-51897-0

1 2 3 4 5 6 7 8 9 10          40          12 11 10 09 08 07 06 05

# Contents

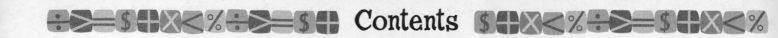

# Contents

The 25 stories in *Fractured Fairy Tales: Math* all have a single purpose: to teach key math topics in an entertaining yet mathematically rigorous context. The stories themselves are based on familiar fairy tales, fables, and related concepts. However, they've all been transformed into something new and, we hope, very funny. For example, Tom Thumb goes out for the basketball team, while Hansel and Gretel get lost on the Internet, and Uncle Goose shares some of *his* nursery rhymes.

Each story serves as a launching pad into a key mathematical concept. The book begins with rounding and estimating. From there, individual stories move through measurement, ratio and proportion, graphing, exponents, and more. Many activities use visual examples to reinforce students' understanding of the material. Each story provides model problems for students to work through before they begin their own computation.

Simple word problems as well as more complex problem solving exercises are provided throughout the text. Finally, a special emphasis in the book is placed on mental math and estimation, encouraging students to use these skills as checks for all kinds of calculations. You will find a complete answer key that starts on page 58.

We recommend the following ways to use these activities in the classroom:

❖ Whole class participation, in which students or the teacher read the story aloud, solve one or more model problem examples, and then solve problems individually.

❖ Small group participation, in which 2 to 5 individuals work together to master the material.

❖ Individual participation, in which students read the stories and solve the problems on their own.

We encourage students to engage the stories directly by writing their own responses, comments, and/or questions to events that take place in the text. One fun, cross-curricular option might have students write their own "fractured" fairy tales to complement the stories that they have read.

Overall, the stories in this book are intended to appeal to all kinds of learners—including students not easily motivated by traditional textbooks—making math learning fun and accessible for all.

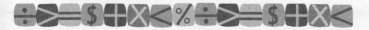 

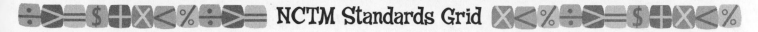
| | Number and Operations | Algebra | Geometry | Measurement | Data Analysis and Probability | Problem Solving | Reasoning and Proof | Communication | Connections | Representation |
|---|---|---|---|---|---|---|---|---|---|---|
| Editorial: Vote for King Uthor the Magnificent | X | | | | | | X | X | X | X |
| Job Openings | X | X | | | X | | X | X | X | X |
| The Acorn and the Pumpkin | X | X | | | | | X | X | X | X |
| Judge Sharko and the Truth Box | X | X | | | | | X | X | X | X |
| Tom Thumb | X | | | | X | X | X | X | X | X |
| City of Underwear | X | | | | X | X | X | X | X | X |
| Interview With the "Lion" King | X | | | X | | | X | X | X | X |
| The Queen of Shapes | X | | | X | | | X | X | X | X |
| Breaking News: Money Found to Grow on Trees! | X | X | | | | X | X | X | X | X |
| The Stolen Shadow, Part 1 | X | X | | | | | X | X | X | X |
| The Stolen Shadow, Part 2 | X | X | | | | | X | X | X | X |
| Advice From Magda | X | | | | | X | X | X | X | X |
| More Advice From Magda | X | | | | | X | X | X | X | X |
| The Most Beautiful Sight in the World | X | | | | | X | X | X | X | X |
| Is Beauty Only Skin Deep? | X | | | | | X | X | X | X | X |
| Channel F Presents: Love at First Sight | X | | | | | X | X | X | X | X |
| Judge Sharko and the Spilled Mush-a-Slush | X | X | | | X | | X | X | X | X |
| Giraffe and Bear Have Dinner | X | X | | | X | | X | X | X | X |
| The Baa Baa Police Report | X | | | | X | | X | X | X | X |
| The Hoop in the Stone | X | | | | X | | X | X | X | X |
| The Leopard in the Cage | X | | | X | | | X | X | X | X |
| Hansel and Gretel, Lost on the Internet | X | | | | | | X | X | X | X |
| The Grand Fool Fest | X | | | | | | X | X | X | X |
| The Prince and the Bakery Boy | X | | | | X | | X | X | X | X |
| Uncle Goose | X | | | | | | X | X | X | X |

Name _____  Date _____

The Fairy Tale World's Greatest Newspaper

# ★ THE FRACTURED ★ FAIRY TALE GAZETTE

VOL. CLIII . . . . No. 55,554          Monday, September 24          $3.00

## Editorial:

### Vote for King Uthor the Magnificent

We at the *Gazette* look forward to the election this week for the office of King and Supreme Ruler. The three candidates are Alfred the Scoundrel, Simpson the Stooge, and, of course, the incumbent, His Royal Highness, Uthor the Magnificent. We have rated the candidates in two categories: Qualifications and Accomplishments.

### QUALIFICATIONS

**Alfred the Scoundrel:** He's a thief and a cheat. He would swindle his own mother and take candy from a baby. Otherwise, he's an excellent candidate.

**Simpson the Stooge:** He's a brainless, spineless, dawdling lazybones. He has no more sense than a woodchuck. Other than that, he's a fine choice.

**His Royal Highness, Uthor the Magnificent:** He's a great leader. Plus, he'll throw us in the dungeon if we don't support him.

### Model

In last year's election, Uthor was the winner in all 147 districts. Round this number to the nearest 10 and 100.

→ Round 147 to the nearest 10.
To round to the nearest 10, look at the ones. Is the number 5 or greater? If yes, round up. If no, round down.
So, rounding up, 147 becomes 150.

→ Round 147 to the nearest 100
To round to the nearest 100, look at the tens. Is the number 5 (50) or greater? If yes, round up. If no, round down.
So, rounding down, 147 becomes 100.

Round to the nearest 10 and the nearest 100.

1. 43     _____     _____

2. 17     _____     _____

3. 121     _____     _____

4. 279     _____     _____

5. 2136     _____     _____

**Name** _____  **Date** _____

## ACCOMPLISHMENTS

**Alfred the Scoundrel:** He's had no accomplishments, unless you count lying, cheating, and stealing.

**Simpson the Stooge:** Zero, zilch, nothing. They don't call him Simpson the Stooge for nothing.

**His Royal Highness, Uthor the Magnificent:** He's collected LOTS of tax money. He's put up dozens of statues of himself. He's created many new jobs.[1] He has maintained a "full-dungeon" policy. Generally, he's improved the lives of thousands![2]

――――――( Model )――――――

In last year's election, Uthor the Magnificent got 81,536 votes in District 1.

Round 81,536 to the nearest 1000 →
  82,000

Round 81,536 to the nearest 10,000 →
  80,000

――――――――――――――――――――

**Round to the nearest 1000 and 10,000.**

6. 2345 _____ _____

7. 4567 _____ _____

8. 19,206 _____ _____

9. 32,494 _____ _____

10. 49,773 _____ _____

11. 453,086 _____ _____

## OUR RECOMMENDATION

**Alfred the Scoundrel:** Are you kidding?

**Simpson the Stooge:** It would be better to have a termite rule the kingdom than to put this loser in office.

**His Royal Highness, Uthor the Magnificent:** After careful consideration, he gets our vote. Why? Because he's honest, loyal, and magnificent, and because he will close down this newspaper and lock us in the dungeon if we don't recommend him. So vote Uthor for this election—*we'll* be glad you did!

12. The election results are in. In District 2, Uthor got 46,754 votes. To the nearest thousand, how many votes did Uthor get?

_____

13. In District 3, Alfred the Scoundrel ended up with 142 votes. To the nearest 10, how many votes did he get?

_____

14. In District 4, Alfred had 233 votes while Simpson the Stooge got 228 votes. Round to the nearest 10. Who got the most votes?

_____

15. In District 5, Alfred had 348 votes while Simpson the Stooge got 351 votes. To the nearest 10, who was ahead? To the nearest 100, who was ahead?

_____

[1] FOR FAMILY MEMBERS AND CLOSE FRIENDS ONLY.
[2] BY SENDING THEM AUTOGRAPHED PICTURES OF HIMSELF.

Name _____ Date _____

The Fairy Tale World's Greatest Newspaper

# ★ THE FRACTURED ★ FAIRY TALE GAZETTE

VOL. CLIII .... No. 55,554                    Monday, September 24                    $3.00

## Job Openings

**ROYAL TASTER** An exciting opportunity for an eager go-getter who doesn't mind being poisoned from time to time. Great food! Your job is to sample the king and queen's food before they eat it. If you turn green and pass out, then they'll know to have something else for dinner.

**PART-TIME FOOL** You: a dunce, an oaf, a bonehead. Your bosses: their Royal Highnesses, the King and Queen. Your duties: keep them laughing—or else! Must be good at: falling down, getting hit in the face with pies. Laughing at King's jokes a must. Master's Degree in Gibberish or Balderdash preferred. Apply in person at the Castle.

**PEASANT** Are you the kind of person who likes to work endless hours for little or no reward? Do you enjoy tilling the soil? Sweating? Grunting and groaning? Being exploited and taken advantage of? Then this is the position for you. Apply at the manor house. No experience necessary.

( Model )

 A fool should expect to fall down about 37 times a day. Over an entire week, how many times would a fool fall down? Estimate.

Round: 37 x 7 → 40 x 7

Multiply & attach zero: 4 x 7 = 28 → 280

First round to find a compatible number. Then use mental math to estimate each answer.

1. 21 x 3 = _____

2. 34 + 42 = _____

3. 58 − 32 = _____

4. 89 ÷ 3 = _____

5. 216 x 4 = _____

6. 193 − 108 = _____

7. 244 ÷ 6 = _____

8. 413 + 295 = _____

9. 484 + 716 = _____

10. 888 − 497 = _____

11. 731 ÷ 8 = _____

Name _____ Date _____

**SWINDLER'S ASSISTANT** Well-known flim-flam man needs a reliable helper who enjoys cheating honest people out of their hard-earned life savings. Must be a fast runner and not mind occasional tarring-and-feathering.

**TRAVELING TROUBADOUR** Sing for your supper. Go from village to village, singing your song. If they like you, you get treated to a wonderful evening. If they don't, get ready to run! The good thing? No matter how bad you are, you're the only entertainment they've got!

( Model )

A traveling troubadour usually visits 23 villages per month. In each village, 37 people hear him sing. How many people hear him sing per month? Estimate.

Round: 23 x 37 → 20 x 40
Multiply without zeroes: 2 x 4 = 8
Attach 2 zeroes: 20 x 40 = 800

Use estimation to find each answer.

**12.** 13 x 52 = _____

**13.** 26 x 33 = _____

**14.** 67 x 45 = _____

**15.** 78 x 63 = _____

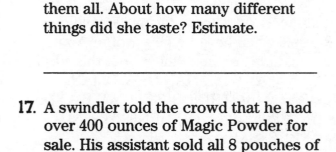

**16.** For the Royal Feast, the cook set out 43 different soups, 26 different meats, 19 different cheeses, and 36 different fishes. The Royal Taster had to taste them all. About how many different things did she taste? Estimate.

_____

**17.** A swindler told the crowd that he had over 400 ounces of Magic Powder for sale. His assistant sold all 8 pouches of Magic Powder. Each pouch contained 53 ounces of Magic Powder. Had the swindler told the truth? Estimate.

_____

Name _____  Date _____

# The Acorn and the Pumpkin

King Phil needed a new advisor. The old one suddenly quit when he got a better offer from another kingdom. So, King Phil put out this ad: WANTED: ROYAL WISE MAN OR WOMAN. DUTIES: SAY WISE THINGS, TELL WISE AND CHARMING TALES. GOOD BENEFITS. NO TYPING NECESSARY.

Many wise men and women came to answer the ad. The king dismissed them all—except for the final two: Omar the Brilliant and Trudy the Fairly Reasonable.

The king looked to Trudy first. "Tell me something wise," he said, "or at least something that is fairly reasonable."

"Nature has more wisdom than we can ever know," Trudy said.

"That sounds reasonable," said the king.

But Omar the Brilliant scoffed.

"Tut tut," said Omar. "This woman is obviously a fool and a fraud. For it is clear—we humans are far more brilliant than nature. And *I* am the most brilliant human being of all."

"You boast well," said the king to Omar. "But what proof do you have of *your* brilliance and nature's folly?"

"Ah," said Omar, pointing above. "Your Majesty need look no farther than this oak tree and this pumpkin plant. The oak is a mighty tree with a mighty trunk and branches. But its acorns are small and modest."

"This is true," said the king. "Big tree. Small acorns."

"The pumpkin, on the other hand," Omar said, "has a mighty fruit but its plant is weak and spindly. Surely this is nature's blunder. A brilliant man like myself would have a much better design."

"How so?" asked Trudy.

"Dear woman," Omar clucked. "It is quite simple. I would put the pumpkin on the mighty oak tree, whose high and mighty branches could support it better. And I would put the tiny acorn on the spindly pumpkin plant, close to the ground."

"It seems a wise idea to me," said the king.

"'Tis better than wise," said Omar. "It is plain brilliant. And if you don't mind, sire, I should now claim the title of Royal Wise Man, for the brilliance I have demonstrated here has most *clearly* earned me that title."

The king looked to Trudy. "What say you?" he asked.

Trudy said nothing, but merely pointed above as a rush of wind moved through the air. A moment later, something fell from the sky: a tiny acorn plopped on the king's head.

"There is my answer," Trudy said. "Had the acorn been a pumpkin, we would now be in search of a new king!"

Even Omar the Brilliant could not deny the reasonableness of this statement. So Trudy the Fairly Reasonable was named to the post of Wise Woman, and a wiser choice King Phil never made.

**THE END**

Name _____ Date _____

---
( Model )
---

Trudy's first official duty as Royal Wise Woman was to help the Royal Soothsayer with his division.

"How can I find out if a number like 129 divides evenly by 3 or 2?" the Royal Soothsayer asked Trudy. Trudy came up with the following rules. She calls them Trudy's Fairly Reasonable Rules for Divisibility.

| Trudy's Fairly Reasonable Rules for Divisibility | | |
|---|---|---|
| A number is divisible by... | If... | Example |
| 2 | the last digit is an even number | 138: 8 is even; 138 ÷ 2 = 69 |
| 3 | the sum of the digits divides evenly by 3 | 126: 1 + 2 + 6 = 9 → 9 ÷ 3 = 3 |
| 4 | the last two digits each divide evenly by 4 | 184: 8 ÷ 4 = 2 and 4 ÷ 4 = 1 |
| 5 | the last digit divides evenly by 5 | 435: 5 ÷ 5 = 1 |
| 6 | the number divides evenly by 3 and by 2 | 438: 4 + 3 + 8 = 15 and 8 is even; 15 ÷ 3 = 5 and 8 ÷ 2 = 4 |
| 9 | the sum of the digits divides evenly by 9 | 675: 6 + 7 + 5 = 18 → 18 ÷ 9 = 2 |
| 10 | the last digit is zero | 340: 340 ÷ 10 = 34 |

1. Which number is divisible by 2?

  (a) 251    (b) 344    (c) 869    (d) 113

2. Which number is divisible by 3?

  (a) 432    (b) 292    (c) 412    (d) 983

3. Which number is divisible by 9?
  (a) 435    (b) 207    (c) 969    (d) 609

4. Which numbers are divisible by 6?

  (a) 114    (b) 363    (c) 448    (d) 876

5. Which numbers are divisible by both 5 and 10?

  (a) 235    (b) 460    (c) 210    (d) 201

6. Which number between 460 and 470 is divisible by 9?

_____

7. True or false? All even numbers are divisible by 2. Give an example.

_____

8. True or false? All odd numbers are divisible by 3. Give an example.

_____

9. True or false? All numbers that are divisible by 9 are also divisible by 3. Give an example.

_____

Name _____   Date _____

## Judge Sharko and the Truth Box

Word got to Judge Sharko that a rival judge in a distant district was using a Truth Box to decide legal cases. Judge Sharko wanted to find out about this so-called Truth Box used by her rival, Judge Merkin. So, Sharko traveled to Merkin's district, disguised as a humble citizen.

In Judge Merkin's court, Sharko got a good view of the Truth Box in action. The first case involved a merchant and a poor farmer. Merkin listened carefully with the Truth Box on his lap. When the merchant spoke, a disk on the Truth Box moved to the space labeled TRUE. When the poor farmer spoke, it moved to the FALSE space.

"The farmer is lying," Judge Merkin declared. "The farmer shall pay a fine and be locked up for three days. The Truth Box never lies."

"This is outrageous!" cried the farmer. Judge Sharko agreed.

Other cases followed. In each, the Truth Box seemed to favor the wealthier citizen. Finally, it was Judge Sharko's turn to speak.

"Your Honor," said the disguised Sharko, "I would hereby like to state that the Truth Box is a fraud."

"This foolish woman insults the great Judge Merkin!" cried the court clerk. "This cannot be allowed!"

### Model

A real Truth Box would show the following properties to be true.

| Identity Properties | Example |
|---|---|
| Addition: $A + O = A$ | $3 + O = 3$ |
| Multiplication: $A \times 1 = A$ | $5 \times 1 = 5$ |

| Commutative Properties | Example |
|---|---|
| Addition: $A + B = B + A$ | $3 + 2 = 2 + 3$ |
| Multiplication: $A \times B = B \times A$ | $4 \times 5 = 5 \times 4$ |

| Zero Property | Example |
|---|---|
| Multiplication by zero: $A \times O = O$ | $4 \times O = O$ |

**Identify each property.**

1. $5 + 7 = 7 + 5$ _____

2. $5 \times 0 = 0$ _____

3. $9 + 0 = 9$ _____

4. $4 \times 1 = 4$ _____

5. $3 \times 6 = 6 \times 3$ _____

**Fill in the blanks and identify each property.**

Property

6. $7 \times \rule{1.5cm}{0.4pt} = 7$ _____

7. $4 + 5 = \rule{1.5cm}{0.4pt} + \rule{1.5cm}{0.4pt}$ _____

8. $8 + \rule{1.5cm}{0.4pt} = 8$ _____

9. $3 \times \rule{1.5cm}{0.4pt} = 2 \times \rule{1.5cm}{0.4pt}$ _____

10. $237 \times 0 = \rule{1.5cm}{0.4pt}$ _____

Name _____  Date _____

"Silence!" said Merkin calmly. "Let the Truth Box determine the truth. You say that the Truth Box is a fraud. Are you telling the truth, woman?"

"No," said Sharko. "I *am* lying. I am a liar, and everything I say is a lie."

This response was not expected. The disk on the Truth Box first moved this way, then that. Finally, it settled on the TRUE space.

Judge Merkin smiled. "Once again, the Truth Box has shown the way," he said. "You are a liar, woman. Everything you say is a lie. The Truth Box confirms this. The Truth Box never lies."

Now Judge Sharko smiled. Merkin had fallen into her trap.

"If everything I say is a lie," she said, "then I must be telling the truth when I admit to being a liar. If that is true, then the Truth Box—*a device that never lies*—is clearly lying. If the Truth Box lies about one thing, it lies about many things."

Here, things fell into a frenzy of shouting and arguing. In the confusion, Judge Sharko managed to approach Judge Merkin and lift the top off the Truth Box. And what did she find? A magnet! Judge Merkin was using a small magnet to drag the Truth Disk toward either the TRUE or FALSE space.

"I hereby declare this Truth Box to be a hoax!" cried Judge Sharko.

To make a long story short, the Governor did not take kindly to Judge Merkin's dishonest ways. The Truth Box was thrown in the trash. Merkin was sentenced to cleaning the judicial stables. Justice was restored.

**THE END**

---

**Model**

Without the help of the "Truth" Box, Judge Sharko was able to confirm three more properties.

**Associative Properties**

Addition: (A + B) + C = A + (B + C)
   Example: (3 + 2) + 4 = 3 + (2 + 4)
Multiplication: (A x B) x C = A x (B x C)
   Example: (5 x 3) x 2 = 5 x (3 x 2)

**Distributive Property**

A x (B + C) = (A x B) + (A x C)
   Example: 3 x (4 + 2) = (3 x 4) + (3 x 2)

---

**Identify each property.**

11. (7 x 5) x 6 = 7 x (5 x 6) _____

12. 8 x (2 + 9) = (8 x 2) + (8 x 9) _____

13. (5 + 3) + 4 = 5 + (3 + 4) _____

**Fill in the blanks.**

14. 3 x (5 + 7) = (3 x _____) + (3 x _____)

15. (4 + 2) + 7 = 4 + (_____ + _____)

16. (7 x 5) x 6 = _____ x (_____ x 6)

Name _____     Date _____

## Tom Thumb

Once there was basketball coach who had a single wish. "I wish the team had at least one player who was seven-feet tall. Then we'd win a championship," he said.

Well, the very next day a new player showed up at the gym. This player was not seven-feet tall—or for that matter, six-feet tall. In fact, this new player was not even five-feet tall.

"How tall are you, son?" the coach asked.

"Four-eleven and three-quarters," the player said.

"That's not very tall for a basketball player," the coach said.

"I'm not very fast, either," said the player, whose name was Tom Thumb. "And I'm not all that great at shooting or passing."

"Do you mind me asking what you *are* good at?" the coach said.

"I can *act*," Tom Thumb said. "I can use my acting skills to make people think I'm taller than I actually am."

The coach rolled his eyes. "Show me," he said.

Tom played, and sure enough, he was able to use his acting skill to give the *illusion* that he was much taller. How tall?

"Seven feet," said one player. "This guy's huge!"

"Amazing!" said the coach.

So Tom Thumb joined the team. And things went splendidly for a while. The team began to win games. The coach began to dream of a championship. Who needed height when you could *act*?

And then it happened. At the beginning of the final championship game, there was a tussle. Tom Thumb went tumbling to the ground. It didn't matter that Tom was a brilliant actor. When a large basketball player lands on someone who is actually only four-foot eleven, there is no denying the result (the smaller player gets squished).

"Are you okay, Tom?" the coach asked his fallen hero.

"I think so," Tom said. But soon it became clear that the fall had damaged his acting ability. Tom began to shrink. Soon, it was obvious that he was no taller than his actual height.

"What am I going to do?" said the coach.

"Put me back in," Tom said. "I may no longer seem tall, but I've still got heart."

Unfortunately, Tom had little else. Tom played with all the skill and heart that he could muster. But truth be told, he played like someone who was four-foot eleven.

The team lost the game. Badly. The dream of a championship was lost. Which just goes to show: even fairy tales can have unhappy endings.

### THE END

### Epilogue

Tom Thumb went to Hollywood, but he didn't make it as an actor. However, Tom's acting ability and basketball experience *did* manage to land him a good job. He became coach of the Hollywood Fakers professional team, and was able to lure several seven-footers to his squad, which won several championships.

Which just goes to show that unhappy endings aren't always as unhappy as you think they are.

Name _____ Date _____

_____ (Model) _____

Look at the diagram of Tom Thumb. Notice his height is measured in feet. Compare his height to that of his shoes, belt, nose, and so on.

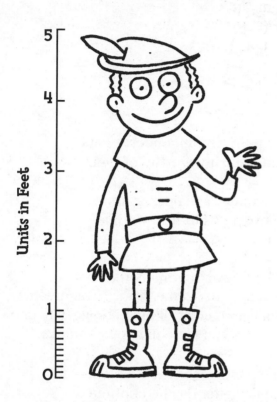

Circle the most reasonable measurements. Refer to the diagram above, if necessary, to help you determine your answer.

1. height of basketball basket

   10 feet     10 inches     20 feet

2. length of a basketball court

   10 feet     144 inches     92 feet

3. length of a referee's whistle

   10 inches   2 inches     3 feet

4. width of a basketball backboard

   8 feet     18 inches     2 feet

5. diameter of a basketball

   3 feet     3 inches     1 foot

What unit of measurement would you use to measure the following, feet or inches?

6. the length of a pencil   _____

7. the length of a car   _____

8. the height of your school building   _____

9. the distance of a city block   _____

10. the length of a hot dog   _____

11. the width of a soccer goal   _____

12. the width of home plate for baseball   _____

13. the length of your classroom   _____

14. the height of a curb   _____

Name _____ Date _____

## City of Underwear

You know the story of the Emperor's New Clothes. Briefly, an emperor gets a suit of clothes that can be seen only by those who are truly worthy of their position in life.

So of course, no one in the emperor's court—including the emperor himself—is willing to say that he or she can't see the emperor's clothes. Until a small child cries out:

*"He's in his underwear!"*

And suddenly one and all can admit: it's a hoax. The reason no one could see the emperor's clothes was that *he wasn't wearing them!*

Recently, a similar situation occurred—except for one key difference: There was no child to call out: *"He's in his underwear!"*

So what happened?

Actually, things turned out to be quite surprising. First, since no one said otherwise, the emperor stayed there in his underwear. And day after day he continued to appear on his royal throne in nothing but underwear.

Now, having a supreme leader walking around in his underwear had an effect on the population. At first people were upset, embarrassed, and disturbed. But after a while, people started to adjust. Over time, a few people even began to *imitate* the style, wearing their own underwear. And soon it began to catch on everywhere. The butcher, the baker, the candlestick-maker—you name it. There they were—all walking around in their underwear!

As one thing led to the next, the city's clothing makers took advantage of the style and began designing *Anywhere Underwear*—underwear that looked good no matter how or where it was worn.

Before long, the kingdom gained significant fame as a fashion capital. Fashion attracted other forms of commerce, and this commerce brought creative people of every stripe—all attracted to the "The Underwear Kingdom."

And they all lived happily ever after—that is, until winter arrived!

**THE END**

Name _____ Date _____

---

### Model

The emperor's waist was 2 feet 8 inches around.
How many inches is this?
Use the chart. Multiply feet by 12. Then add the
extra inches.

| To change . . . | | | |
|---|---|---|---|
| ↓ | inches | feet | yards |
| inches to . . . | -- | divide by 12 | divide by 36 |
| feet to . . . | multiply by 12 | -- | divide by 3 |
| yards to . . . | multiply by 36 | multiply by 3 | -- |

2 ft 8 in → First multiply: 2 x 12 = 24
Then add: 8 → 24 + 8 = 32 inches

_____

**Use the chart to find the following.**

1. 3 ft = _____ in

2. 1 ft 6 in = _____ in

3. 6 ft 4 in = _____ in

4. 48 in = _____ ft

5. 84 in = _____ ft

6. 108 in = _____ yd

7. 3 yd 5 in = _____ in

8. 60 ft = _____ yd

9. 5 yd = _____ in

10. The streets in the City of Underwear are 14
yards wide. How many feet is this? How many
inches is this?

_____

11. The emperor's pants are 4 feet 6 inches in
length. How many inches is this?

_____

12. The emperor built a tower that was 855 feet
tall. How many yards was this?

_____

13. How many inches tall is the 855-foot high
tower?

_____

Name _____     Date _____

## Interview With the "Lion" King

*Hello, and welcome to Channel F, the Fairy Tale Channel. I'm Pillow Jones, your host. Tonight on F, an interview with the "Lion" King*

**Pillow:** Good evening, Your Highness. Let me begin. There are rumors that suggest you can't be a real "Lion" King. What's your response?

**LK:** If I'm not really a lion, then why do I have this lion's mane on my head?

**Pillow:** With all due respect, that's not a lion's mane. It's a Detroit Lions baseball cap.

**LK:** Well, can you blame a fellow for trying? Anyway, for the record, I never claimed to be an actual lion, that is, King of the Jungle. All I said was that I was a *Line* King.

**Pillow:** A *Line* King? What's a *Line* King?

**LK:** Well, in my case, as a Line King, I am interested in lines.

**Pillow:** Lines? What kind of lines? Straight lines? Crooked lines? Perpendicular lines? Parallel lines? Rays? Segments?

**LK:** All of the above. And figures, too. Right now I'm supporting a new law that says: Parallel lines shall never meet.

**Pillow:** And what happens to parallel lines that insist on meeting?

**LK:** I see three options. Either have them declared to be intersecting lines or have them classified as perpendicular lines.

**Pillow:** That's two. What's the third option?

**LK:** Have them thrown in the dungeon.

**Pillow:** You would throw perfectly parallel lines into the dungeon, just because they tried to meet? Isn't that a bit harsh?

**LK:** I don't think so. After all, what are parallel lines if they meet? They're certainly not parallel.

**Pillow:** You've got a point there. What about perpendicular lines?

**LK:** I think they should meet at 90 degrees. And I would support a law stating that the shortest distance between any two points is a straight line.

**Pillow:** A straight line? What does that say to all the crooked lines and curved lines out there?

**LK:** Hey, I try to be fair. But there are some things even a Line King can't do.

**Pillow:** Fascinating. Anything else you'd like to say about lines?

**LK:** Yes. With respect to grocery store and movie ticket lines, I support legislation that would make it illegal to cut in front of someone in line, unless that person is a friend or a family member.

**Pillow:** A splendid idea. Any closing sentiments you'd like to convey to your constituents?

**LK:** Yes. R-R-R-OOOO-ARRR!

**Pillow:** Thank you very much, Your Highness.

**LK:** Thank you, Pillow.

**THE END**

Name _____ Date _____

Using the letters, match the figures on the
right to the descriptions on the left. Use each
answer only once.

**A.**

1. parallel lines          _____

**B.**

2. perpendicular lines     _____

3. rays forming a right angle    _____

**C.**

4. rays forming an acute angle   _____

**D.**

5. intersecting line segments    _____

6. parallel line segments   _____

**E.**

7. nonintersecting lines   _____

**F.**

8. nonparallel lines   _____

Name _____  Date _____

## The Queen of Shapes

Queen Mona the Wise was fond of figures, so she organized a Festival of Shapes. Some of the land's most powerful princes and ministers came to compete to see who could present the finest shape.

Princess Tetragon from the Land of Quadrilateral was first.

"Greetings, Your Highness," she said, bowing humbly. "As you know, I come from a land of many four-sided shapes. Some are small; some are large; but all are excellent—and I intend to show you the very finest shape in the world."

"Proceed," said the Queen, showing keen interest.

"There is only one shape perfect enough for Your Royal Highness," the princess continued. "I'm speaking of a quadrilateral so exquisite that all four of its sides have *exactly* the same length, and all four of its angles have *precisely* the same measure, not one degree more or less."

"Your quadrilateral sounds quite impressive," said the Queen. "May I see it?"

But before the princess could present the shape, the Duke of Diamonds cut in.

"Excuse me, Your Highness," he said, "but I hail from the Land of Parallelogram, and the shape that this princess speaks of sounds like one of our own parallelograms."

"Is this true?" asked the Queen. "Can a parallelogram also be a quadrilateral?"

But before the Duke could answer, Lady Box from the Land of Rectangle cut in.

"I have no doubt that this shape is a rectangle!" she insisted.

Which was followed by Lord Rhombus himself.

"Nonsense!" he cried. "It is a rhombus as sure as I stand here!"

The Queen turned to the fifth and final petitioner. This was a small and sharply angled man—the Sultan of Square.

"There can be no question," he said, in a sharp, high-pitched voice. "The shape they describe is undoubtedly a square. All else is nonsense!"

---

( Model )

Princess Tetragon comes from the Land of Quadrilateral. Which of these shapes come from her land?

(a) _____  (b) _____

(c) _____  (d) _____

### Shapes

3 sides: triangle
4 sides: quadrilateral
5 sides: pentagon
6 sides: hexagon
8 sides: octagon

Shape b is the only quadrilateral because it has 4 sides.

---

Name each shape.

1. _____

2. _____

3. _____

4. _____

5. _____

6. _____

Fractured Fairy Tales: Math • Scholastic Teaching Resources

**Name** _____  **Date** _____

At this, all five of the petitioners took to squabbling and quarreling. Each accused the others of lying.

"He's lying!" said one.

"No, *she's* lying!" said a second.

"*They're all* lying!" said the third.

The only thing that they could all agree on was that only one of them could be telling the truth. Queen Mona, however, disagreed.

"Perhaps *all* of you are telling the truth," the queen said.

"But how could that be?" they cried. How could a *single shape* in fact be *many* shapes?"

This, indeed, was a puzzle. Can you explain how Queen Mona could be correct?

### THE END

**Use the definitions below to answer the questions.**

**Quadrilateral: 4-sided figure**

**Trapezoid: quadrilateral with 1 pair of parallel sides**

**Parallelogram: quadrilateral with 2 pairs of parallel sides and 2 pairs of congruent sides**

**Rectangle: Parallelogram with 4 right angles**

**Rhombus: Parallelogram with 4 congruent sides**

**Square: Rhombus with 4 right angles**

7. What makes Princess Tetragon's shape a quadrilateral?

_____

8. Is Princess Tetragon's shape a parallelogram? Why?

_____

9. Is Princess Tetragon's shape a trapezoid? Why?

_____

10. Is Princess Tetragon's shape a rectangle? Why?

_____

11. Is Princess Tetragon's shape a rhombus? Why?

_____

12. Is Princess Tetragon's shape a square? Why?

_____

13. What kind of a figure is Princess Tetragon's shape? How can Princess Tetragon's shape be a quadrilateral, a parallelogram, a rectangle, a rhombus, and a square all at the same time? Explain.

_____

_____

_____

Name _____   Date _____

### The Fairy Tale World's Greatest Newspaper

# ★ THE FRACTURED ★ FAIRY TALE GAZETTE

VOL. CLIII .... No. 55,554          Monday, September 24          $3.00

## Breaking News:
## Money Found to Grow on Trees!

The Enchanted Forest—In a surprise discovery, money was found growing on trees in the forest last week. Explorer Marge Pockets discovered trees that grow five-, ten-, twenty-, and even 100-dollar bills.

"The larger bills are found higher up," Pockets said.

It also appeared that some branches make change for branches growing above or below them. For example, a 25-cent branch might have two dimes and a nickel growing beneath.

When asked how her discovery might affect the economy, Pockets said, "This will primarily affect the experts who say, '*Money doesn't grow on trees.*'"

Indeed, when asked about the discovery, banker and financier David Dunn-Greed said: "It's true. Money doesn't grow on trees."

When told "*Yes, it does,*" Dunn-Greed replied: "Well, I've been saying it for over thirty years, and I'm not about to stop now." As if to prove it, Dunn-Greed paused, then he repeated, "Money doesn't grow on trees, you know."

### Model

The lower branches make change in $50, $20, $10, $5, or $1 bills for the value of the top branch. What are the missing bills in the third row?

The total of the Row 3 (and all rows) must equal $100, so: $50 + $20 + $20 + $10 = $100

1. Complete Row 4 using one $20 bill.

_____

2. Complete Row 4 using two $20 bills.

_____

3. Complete Row 5 using a $50 bill.

_____

4. Complete Row 5 using no $20 bills.

_____

Name _____  Date _____

In a related story, delighted children reported gumdrops falling from the sky in bright candy colors.

When asked about the finding, weather reporter Slush Peterson said:

"I think it's magic, plain and simple."

When reminded that weather reporters don't believe in magic, Peterson added, "Oh, you're right. So the gumdrops must not be real." At that point a red gumdrop fell directly on Peterson's nose. When asked to explain it, Peterson said:

"What, *this*? This is just a very big raindrop. This is not a gumdrop. No way."

At this point, a young child came and snatched the so-called "rain drop" and popped it into her mouth.

"Candy!" the girl said.

"Hmm," Peterson was heard to add. "Perhaps it is magic after all."

More on this story as it develops.

### THE END

───( Model )───

**Think about the pattern you see for this arrangement of gumdrops.**

1st Row   ⬭

2nd Row   ⬭   ⬭

3rd Row   ⬭   ⬭   ⬭

4th Row   ⬭   ⬭   ⬭   ⬭

**Next, make a table.**

| Row | Gumdrops in row | Total | Sum total + gumdrops in next row |
|-----|-----------------|-------|----------------------------------|
| 1 | 1 | 1 | 1 + 2 = 3 |
| 2 | 2 | 3 | 3 + 3 = 6 |
| 3 | 3 | 6 | 6 + 4 = 10 |
| 4 | 4 | 10 | 10 + ? = ? |
| 5 | | | |
| 6 | | | |

**Continue the table.**

5. How many gumdrops will be in the Row 5? With 5 full rows, what will the total number of gumdrops be?

_____

6. How many gumdrops will be in Row 6? What will the total number of gumdrops be at this point?

_____

7. Finally, describe the pattern of this table. How can you use the pattern to tell what the next number will be?

_____

**Name** _____    **Date** _____

## The Stolen Shadow, Part 1

One day a boy was playing by the river when he suddenly felt something missing.

"My shadow!" the boy cried. "It's gone! Who took my shadow?"

"Why don't you go ask the sun?" said the snake, who was slithering nearby.

So the boy went to the sun.

"Excuse me, golden sun," said the boy. "I am a small boy, and I seemed to have misplaced my shadow. Have you, by any chance, taken it?"

"TAKEN YOUR SHADOW?" thundered the sun. "I could melt you in a minute. Why would I take the shadow of a small boy?"

"Because you have no shadow of your own," said the boy.

"Hmm," snorted the sun. "You've got a point there. But I haven't seen your shadow. Why don't you go ask the moon."

So the boy went to the moon.

"Hello, silver moon," he said.

"Hello, young boy," said the moon. "What brings you out in the night?"

"It is my shadow," said the boy. "Have you seen it? It's not very much bigger than this," he said, holding his hands out wide.

The moon had a musical laugh. "I am a very important part of the sky," she said. "Why would I take the shadow of a boy?"

"Because your own shadow is seen only once a year," said the boy, "when you pass in front of the sun."

"Hmm," said the moon. "That is true. But I haven't seen your shadow. Why don't you go ask the clouds."

So the boy went to the clouds. "Excuse me," he said, "Would you by any chance have noticed the shadow of an insignificant boy? It's much MUCH less important than your own magnificent shadows, of course."

"We *are* quite puffy and magnificent," murmured the clouds. "And *you* are quite small and spindly. Why would we want your shadow?"

"Because your own shadows get in the way of one another," said the boy convincingly. "Perhaps you would like to see just one shadow at a time."

"Hmm," said the clouds. "Perhaps. But that does not mean we would go so low as to steal a boy's shadow. Why don't you go ask the trees."

**To be continued . . .**

─────────( Model )─────────

**The boy is 5-feet tall. His shadow measures 10 feet in length. What is the ratio of the boy to his shadow?**

**The ratio of the boy to his shadow is 5 to 10.**

**The ratio may be written as 5:10 or as the fraction $\frac{5}{10}$. Then simplify if possible.**

$$5{:}10 = \frac{5}{10} = \frac{1}{2}$$

─────────────────────────

**Identify the ratio, fraction, and decimal in the problems below. Remember to simplify where possible.**

1. The snake is 4-feet long and the boy is 5-feet tall. What is the ratio of the boy's height to the snake's length? Write your answer as:

   (a) a ratio _____

   (b) a fraction _____

   (c) a decimal number _____

**Name** _____ **Date** _____

**2.** The cat has a 6-inch head and a 20-inch body. What is the ratio of its head to its body? Write your answer as:

(a) a ratio _____

(b) a fraction _____

(c) a decimal number _____

**3.** If a boy is 60 inches tall and his cat has a length of 24 inches. What is the ratio of the cat to the boy? Write your answer as:

(a) a ratio _____

(b) a fraction _____

(c) a decimal number _____

**4.** Circle any ratio that is equal to the boldfaced ratio on the left.

**3 to 1**     4 to 2     9:3     3.1 to 1     15:5

**5.** Circle any fraction that is equal to the boldfaced ratio on the left.

**4:6**     6/9     2/5     2/3     9/15

**6.** A 4-inch leaf has a shadow of 24 inches. What is the ratio of the shadow of the leaf?

_____

**7.** A cloud measures 40 feet across. Its shadow is 25 feet across. What is the ratio of the cloud to the shadow?

_____

**8.** The river is 120 feet wide and 80 feet deep. What is the ratio of the river's width to its depth?

_____

**9.** A boy swam 60 meters in 40 seconds. What is the ratio of meters to seconds? Of seconds to meters?

_____

Name _____   Date _____

## The Stolen Shadow, Part 2

*A boy lost his shadow near the river. He went to ask the sun where it was. The sun didn't know. He asked the moon where it was. The moon didn't know. He asked the clouds where it was. The clouds also didn't know. But the clouds suggested that the boy go to the trees.*

"Hello, rustling cousins," the boy said to the trees. "Would you have noticed a small boy's shadow wandering about? I need it very much."

"Your shadow does not flutter and ripple like our own shadows," answered the trees. "Of what use would it be to us?"

"My shadow may not flutter and ripple," the boy said. "But unlike yours, it can travel from one place to another."

"My," said the trees. "You are a smart boy. But we have no idea where your shadow is. Why don't you go ask the river."

So the boy went back to the river.

"I know this sounds silly, shimmering sister," he said. "I am looking for my shadow. Last I saw it I was right here—near your banks."

The river had the best laugh of all: "Bub-ub-ub-ub-ub-ub!" she gurgled. "Mine is a dancing, darting, flickering shadow. Why would I want a shadow that cannot dance, dart, or flicker?"

"Hmm," thought the boy. "Perhaps because your shadow is not really a shadow. It is only a reflection."

"Bub-ub-ub!" cried the river. "You are an intelligent boy indeed. I do not have your shadow, but here is some advice: Go see that rascally snake."

"*The snake!*" the boy cried. "Of course. *He* must have taken my shadow all along!"

The boy went to find the snake who was digesting a VERY large meal.

"Ugh!" said the snake. "What brings you back here, troublesome boy. Can't you see I'm busy digesting?"

"Hello, slithering brother," said the boy. "Hand over my shadow. You've had it the whole time."

"Not so fast," said the snake. "It's true—I *did* take your shadow. It looked so dark and beautiful I could not help but borrow it for awhile. But then the cat saw me playing with it. And she offered me a fine meal if I gave the shadow to her."

"But why would a cat want a boy's shadow?" said the boy. "Unlike you, slithering brother, the cat has her own shadow."

"See for yourself," said the snake.

And there was the cat, playing in the sunshine with not one but TWO shadows—a *cat* shadow and a *boy* shadow. The two shadows were chasing one another.

"Hey!" cried the boy.

He ran to retrieve his stolen shadow. But on the way, the snake raised his tail, just a bit, which tripped the boy, causing him to crash into the cat, dislodging one of the shadows.

"R-R-RA-YAAAAA-L-LLLLL!" hissed the cat.

Luckily, the freed shadow was the one that belonged to the boy.

"Welcome home, good friend," the boy said to his shadow.

And it fit just perfectly.

**THE END**

**Name** _____ **Date** _____

---

( **Model** )

The boy standing next to a tree is 5 feet tall. His shadow is 10 feet in length. If the tree is 30 feet in height, what is the length of the tree's shadow?

Cross multiply. Then divide to find the answer.

$$\frac{5}{10} \times \frac{30}{?}$$

10 x 30 = 300; 300 ÷ 5 = 60

The tree's shadow is 60 feet.

---

1. Circle the quantities that are equal to the bold-faced ratio.

   **5 to 2**    $\frac{15}{6}$    10:3    2.5 to 1    10:8

2. Circle the quantities that are equal to the bold-faced ratio.

   **9:4**    2.5 to 1    $\frac{4}{9}$    $\frac{9}{4}$    $2\frac{1}{4}$ to 1

3. A boy is 5-feet tall and a man is 6-feet tall. If the boy's shadow measures 10 feet across, how long is the man's shadow?

   _____

4. If a boy swims 60 meters in 40 seconds, how far would he swim in 50 seconds?

   _____

5. The ratio of a cat to its shadow is 1 to 3.5. If the cat's tail is 14 inches in length, how long is the cat's shadow's tail?

   _____

6. Using the ratio in problem 5, if the cat's ear is 1.6 inches in height, what is the height of the shadow of the cat's ear?

   _____

7. In length, the ratio of a boy's leg to his foot is 2.5 to 1. If the boy's foot is 9 inches in length, how long is his leg?

   _____

8. Lion was hiding behind a 12-foot bush. The bush had a 30-foot shadow. Lion's shadow was 16 feet in height. How tall was lion?

   _____

9. The ratio of a mountain to its shadow was 4 to 1. The mountain is 2000 feet tall. How tall is its shadow?

   _____

Name _____   Date _____

## Advice From Magda, the King's Royal Seer and Mystic

Dear Magda,

Recently, I went up a hill with a friend named Jack to fetch a pail of water. Jack fell down. He ended up breaking his crown. But the thing is, I came tumbling after. Now Jack says it was all my fault. He wants to sue me. Can he?

Signed, Jill

Dear Jill,

The key question is, whose idea was it to fetch the pail of water? If it was his, you're in the clear. If it was yours, give up, honey, before you really suffer a tumble!

Sincerely, Magda

Dear Magda,

Recently, I've noticed many princesses who are in need of kisses so they may be released from one spell or another. I was wondering, though I'm not really a prince and I'm not really handsome, would it be okay if I went around kissing these princesses anyway? I mean, what could it hurt?

Signed, Good Kisser

Dear Good,

Nice try, but sorry. Each magic spell states clearly that the princess must be kissed by a genuine "handsome prince." Your only hope is to get a really good lawyer who could reword the magic spell to say "ordinary commoner" instead of "handsome prince."
Good luck.

Sincerely, Magda

Dear Magda,

Recently, I was saved from a burning castle tower by a knight in shining armor. Now that I'm saved, this knight wants to get married and live happily ever after. The truth is, he's a nice enough guy, but I don't feel any magic there. What do I owe this guy?

Signed, Damsel No Longer in Distress

Dear Damsel,

Not much! I can't tell you how many bad relationships start out because someone gets saved from a burning tower. Don't do it, honey!

Sincerely, Magda

**Name** _____ **Date** _____

( Model )

In which year did the greatest number of damsels get saved? How many damsels got saved that year?

**Damsels Saved From Burning Towers**

**Answer:** In 1068, 19 damsels were saved.

_____

1. What years does this graph cover?

_____

2. During which year were 16 damsels saved?

_____

3. How many damsels were saved in 1066?

_____

4. During which year were the fewest number of damsels saved?

_____

5. Between what years was the greatest increase in saved damsels?

_____

6. After which years did the number of saved damsels decrease?

_____

7. In which years were the same number of damsels saved?

_____

8. Between which years was there the least amount of change in the number of damsels saved? Circle your answer.

1064–1065          1066–1067          1068–1069

Name _____ Date _____

## More Advice From Magda, the King's Royal Seer and Mystic

Dear Magda,

Recently, I brought the king bad news. He had me locked up in the dungeon. Isn't this what's referred to as "shooting the messenger"?

Signed, Dungeon Joe

Dear DJ,

No, simply put, it's called locking up the messenger in the dungeon.

Sincerely, Magda

Dear Magda,

Recently, I've lost my taste for porridge. Whether it's too hot, too cold, or just right, I'm just plain sick of the stuff. Since I don't cook, I've always relied on the Three Bears for my meals. What should I do now?

Signed, Goldie

Dear Goldie,

My advice is to try to mix it up a bit. No one can eat the same thing day after day! Better yet—learn to cook!

Sincerely, Magda

Dear Magda,

Recently, an evil sorcerer turned my cousin into a toad. Now I find that this same sorcerer and I have been invited to a dinner party and we're even going to sit next to each other. Should I be nice?

Signed, Toad-ly Upset

Dear Toad-ly,

You'd better, or he'll turn you into a donkey!

Sincerely, Magda

Name _____     Date _____

─────────────── (Model) ───────────────

**What was the most popular animal that sorcerers turned people into last year?**

Bar graph with y-axis from 0 to 100 (marked in 10s) and x-axis categories: Donkey (20), Mouse (30), Fish (40), Frog or Toad (95), Chicken (15), Pig (45).

**Answer: The most popular animal was a frog or toad.**

1. How many people were turned into frogs or toads?

_____

2. What was the least popular animal?

_____

3. Together, the number of mice and chickens was about equal to the number of what animal?

_____

4. How many more people were turned into pigs than were turned into fish?

_____

5. How many people were turned into animals in all?

_____

6. Rounded to the nearest tenth, what percentage of the total number of animals is represented by frogs and toads?

_____

7. Which two groups together make up about one-third of the total number of animals?

_____

8. A sorcerer turned a prince into an animal. What are the chances that he will be either a mouse or a fish?

_____

**Name** _____  **Date** _____

# The Most Beautiful Sight in the World

Queen Mona the Wise was a leader who liked to ask challenging questions. One afternoon she invited an artist, a musician, a bricklayer, and a fool to a small banquet. Before the refreshments were served, the conversation got around to a challenging topic.

*What was the most beautiful sight in the world?*

All of the guests were great talkers, so rather than distract themselves with lunch, they sent the food platters away and debated the subject. Hours passed without any conclusion. Finally the queen and demanded that each guest state a position. The guest with the most convincing answer would receive a special royal reward.

The queen began with the artist.

"The most beautiful sight in the world?" the artist said. "Rather than tell you, I will show you." And with that she took a painting out of her satchel. It showed the sun in a glorious blue sky. "I painted it myself," she added.

"Your painting is lovely indeed," said the queen. "But is it the most beautiful sight in the world?" She turned to the musician.

The graph shows which scenes in paintings people found to be most beautiful. Which scene did people think was most beautiful?

**Most Beautiful Painting in the World**
Number of people who voted for each scene

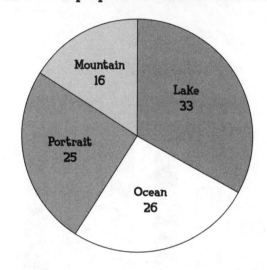

**Answer:** The lake scene was judged to be most beautiful.

_____

**1.** How many votes did the lake scene get?

_____

**2.** How many votes were there in all?

_____

**3.** What fraction of the total vote did the lake scene receive?

_____

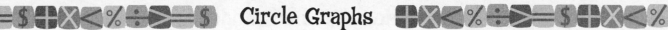

## Circle Graphs

**Name** _____  **Date** _____

**4.** What percent of the votes did the lake scene receive?

_____

**5.** About what fraction of the total vote did the ocean scene receive?

_____

**6.** Which two scenes received about half of the total?

_____

"Her painting is extraordinary," said the musician. "But I have something even more beautiful." Here, she took out her lute and played an enchanting melody.

"Your song is exquisite," said the queen. "But is it the most beautiful thing in the world?"

She turned to the bricklayer.

"The most beautiful sight?" he said. "Simply look out the window. There you can see the tower I have built with my own hands. It is surely the world's most beautiful sight."

"Your tower is a thing of great splendor," said the queen. "But is it more beautiful than all other sights?" She turned to the fool.

At this point, a great deal of time had passed since the five of them had first gathered. They had skipped lunch and missed supper as well. The sun was long down and none of them had had even so much as a morsel to eat or a drop to drink.

"The most beautiful sight in the world?" the fool said. Then he scampered out of the room. In a moment, he returned from the kitchen with a steaming pot of stew.

"Here it is!" the fool cried.

And they all knew it was true. To a person with an empty stomach, there is no sight more beautiful than food.

**THE END**

**Number of people who voted for each food**

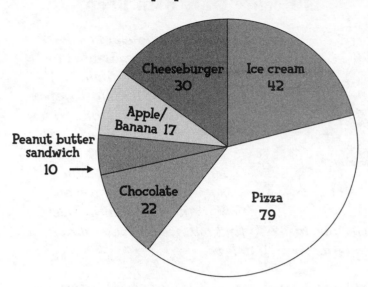

**7.** Which food got the most votes?

_____

**8.** How many votes were there in all?

_____

**9.** About what fraction of the total vote did ice cream receive?

_____

**10.** About what fraction of the total vote did pizza receive?

_____

**11.** Which two categories combined received about $\frac{1}{4}$ of the total?

_____

Name _____     Date _____

## Is Beauty Only Skin Deep?

*This is Pillow Jones, host of Bed-Time Live: Behind the Fairy Tales. Tonight, BTL asks one of the most important questions of our time: Is beauty only skin deep? To find out, we've hired a sorcerer to turn a handsome prince into a toad. Will the beautiful princess still love him? To find out, we've installed hidden cameras. Let's listen in:*

**Princess:** My darling, isn't it wonderful to be together?

**Prince:** Yes!

*A sorcerer casts his spell*

**Princess:** (*gasping*) Oh my, you've turned into an ugly toad!

**Prince:** (*in a croaky voice*) Do you still love me, darling?

**Princess:** Uh, just a second. I need to call my agent.

*Several hours later, the princess finally gets off the phone . . .*

**Princess:** Okay, I've talked it over with my agent and here's the deal. I still love you, but I'm going to be very very busy for the next several months.

**Prince:** Doing what?

**Princess:** Uh, my agent says I have some engagements.

**Pillow:** So our prince and princess have begun their new life together. Will things work out? We'll came back in a few months with our hidden cameras to find out.

---

( Model )

BTL asked a studio audience to rate how important beauty is from 1 to 10. The results are shown. What are the mean, median, and mode of this data?

Data: 4, 7, 4, 8, 5, 10, 4, 9, 3

**Mean**
Total ÷ number of scores: $54 ÷ 9 = 6$

**Median**
Put the data in numerical order and find the central score: 10, 9, 8, 7, 5, 4, 4, 4, 3 → 5

**Mode**
Most common score: 4

---

Use the following data to answer the questions.

11, 17, 16, 12, 14, 9, 18, 15, 14

1. What is the mean?

_____

2. What is the median?

_____

3. What is the mode?

_____

**Name** _____  **Date** _____

*Three months later . . .*

**Prince:** Why are you so cranky all the time?

**Princess:** It's that look on your face. I can't stand that look.

**Prince:** I'm a toad. What other look can I have?

**Princess:** I don't know. Try something different. Something less—

**Prince:** Toadlike?

**Princess:** Yes. There, I've said it. Are you happy now?

**Prince:** No, I'm not happy. I'm a *toad!*

**Pillow:** Now, for some analysis, we bring in castle psychologist and all-around know-it-all, Elvar the Nag. Elvar?

**Elvar:** Well, it appears that *beauty really is only skin deep*—especially if the skin you're talking about is green and bumpy!

**Pillow:** What about for people who aren't green or bumpy?

**Elvar:** *That's* another question, Pillow, and one I can't really answer. What I can definitely tell you is that it's *harder to fall in love with a toad than with a handsome prince. Unless you yourself are a toad, that is!*

**Pillow:** Thank you, Elvar the Nag. So there you have it. Has *BTL* answered the question *Is beauty only skin deep?* Perhaps. Or perhaps questions like this just can't be answered by hidden cameras and other sophisticated technology. Instead, they need to be answered by the human heart, one heart at a time.

**THE END**

Eleven people met the Prince both before and after he was turned into a toad and gave him these scores.

**Appearance**

→ **Before:** 8, 9, 8, 10, 7, 8, 5, 10, 9, 8, 9

→ **After:** 2, 1, 3, 6, 2, 0, 4, 0, 1, 3, 0

Calculate. Round to the nearest hundredth, if necessary.

**4.** What was the Prince's mean "before" score?

_____

**5.** What was the Prince's mean "after" score?

_____

**6.** Compare the mean "before" and "after" scores. By how much did the Prince's rating change?

_____

**7.** Compare the median scores for "before" and "after." By how much did the median score change?

_____

**8.** Compare the mode scores for "before" and "after." By how much did the mode score change?

_____

Name _____

Date _____

## Channel F Presents: Love at First Sight

*Welcome to* Love at First Sight *on Channel F, the Fairy Tale Channel. I'm Pillow Jones, your host. Now let's meet our first contestant, Angie of Fort Worth, Texas. Hi Angie, and welcome to* Love at First Sight. *Are you ready to play?*

**Angie**: Hi Pillow. I'm psyched. This is really going to be great.

**Pillow**: As you know, the rules of our game are simple. We put YOU in our sound-proof LOVE CHAMBER booth.

**Angie**: Oooh, that sounds like fun.

**Pillow**: Then you spin the Prince Spinner to get your choice of handsome prince[1]—Prince A, B, C, D, or E.

**Angie**: That sounds easy. Then what?

**Pillow**: Then you spin the Thumb Spinner. Thumbs Up means it's love at first sight. You and your prince get married and live happily ever after.

**Angie**: And Thumbs Down?

**Pillow**: You don't marry the prince, and you don't live happily ever after.

**Angie**: What do I win?

**Pillow**: Win? You don't win anything.

**Angie**: You mean I don't get anything? No refrigerators or steak knives or dinner at the Moki Loki Lounge or *anything*?

**Pillow**: No.

[1] **Actual handsomeness of *your* prince may vary.**

---

( Model )

What is the probability that Angie's prince will be a dreamboat? Spin the Prince Spinner.

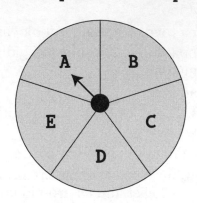

There are five princes . . .
Prince A: a dreamboat
Prince B: a tugboat
Prince C: a little weird
Prince D: very weird
Prince E: works at Burger Town

Only one prince is a dreamboat, so:
$$P\ (\text{dreamboat}) = \frac{1}{5}$$

---

1. What is the probability that Angie's prince will be either a dreamboat or a tugboat?

_____

2. What is the probability that Angie's prince will be just a little weird?

_____

3. What is the probability that Angie's prince will be a little weird or very weird?

_____

Name _____    Date _____

**4.** What is the probability that Angie's prince will not be weird at all?

_____

**5.** What is the probability that Angie will NOT get Prince A on the first spin?

_____

**6.** What is the probability that Angie's spin will land on Prince F?

_____

**Angie:** Suppose I don't like my young prince?

**Pillow:** Spin the Prince Spinner again, and hope you get someone more to your liking.

**Angie:** What if I don't like ANY of the princes?

**Pillow:** I'm sorry, Angie, we have no more time to answer questions. It's time to spin the Prince Spinner. Are you ready, Angie?

*Angie spins, reluctantly.*

**Pillow:** Round and round it goes. And where it stops, nobody knows. Will Angie's prince be the man of her dreams? Oh, that's all we have time for tonight, folks! Tune in next week!

**THE END**

---

( Model )

Suppose Angie spins the Thumb Spinner after she spins the Prince Spinner. What is the probability that she will get Prince A and Thumbs Up?

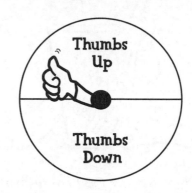

$$P(A \text{ and } Up) = \frac{1}{5} \times \frac{1}{2} = \frac{1}{10}$$

---

To answer the following questions, refer to the models on page 38 and 39.

**7.** In two spins, what is the probability that Angie's will land on Prince A, then Thumbs Down?

_____

**8.** What is the probability that Angie will get Prince A or Prince B on the first spin and Thumbs Up on the second spin?

_____

**9.** What is the probability that Angie will get Prince C, Prince D, or Prince E on the first spin and Thumbs Down on the second spin?

_____

Name _____   Date _____

## Judge Sharko and the Spilled Mush-a-Slush

Judge Sharko never tires of telling of cases in which she got the better of her shady rival, Judge Merkin. One such case involved a young woman named Cricket, who was walking in the market one sunny morning, sipping a Mango-Banana Mush-a-Slush.

Now, a Mush-a-Slush is a kind of wet, messy drink, especially when poured over a person's head. And that is precisely what happened to Cricket. One moment she was standing there, minding her own business.

And the next moment, a well-dressed young man, a complete stranger, came up, grabbed the Mush-a-Slush, and dumped it over Cricket's head, no questions asked.

And what did Cricket do next? What *could* she do? She gasped. It was only then that the young man realized he'd made a mistake.

"Oh sorry," he said to Cricket. "I thought you were someone else." And with that, he disappeared into the crowd.

"*Thought I was someone else*?" cried an outraged Cricket.

"You've got to report this," said a bystander.

Indeed, Cricket did report it. After all, the spilled Mush-a-Slush had ruined her coat, dress, purse, shoes—everything! Plus, it made her late to work. All in all, it ended up ruining an entire day!

---

( Model )

Cricket was 2 hours and 43 minutes late to work. How many minutes was this?

> 1 minute = 60 seconds
> 1 hour = 60 minutes
> 1 day = 24 hours
> 1 week = 7 days
> 1 year = 52 weeks
> 1 year = 365 days

2 hr 43 min = (2 x 60) + 43
            = 120 + 43 = 163 minutes

Cricket spent 94 minutes cleaning her clothing. How many hours was this?

94 ÷ 60 = 1 R 34 = 1 hour 34 minutes

---

**Convert each time.**

1. 100 minutes = _____ hr _____ min

2. 1 hour 37 minutes = _____ min

3. 3 hours 5 minutes = _____ min

4. 431 minutes = _____ hr _____ min

5. 26 hours = _____ d _____ hr

6. 2 days 7 hours = _____ hr

7. 6 days 13 hours = _____ hr

Name _____ Date _____

8. 3 weeks 4 days = _____ d

9. 100 days = _____ wk _____ d

10. 75 weeks = _____ yr _____ wk

11. 8 years 100 days = _____ d

12. 1000 days = _____ yr _____ d

And the young man? His name was Mr. Blunt, and he turned out to be a friend of Judge Merkin.

Though Mr. Blunt was absent from the proceedings, Merkin listened carefully to Mr. Blunt's lawyer. Then the judge made his ruling:

"Your client is ordered to bring one dollar to this courtroom tomorrow," Merkin told the lawyer. "The dollar will pay this young woman for the drink she lost."

"One dollar!" Cricket cried. Was her entire day worth no more than a *single dollar*?

As she left the courtroom, Cricket could not help but wonder: *Was there any justice in the world*? She would find out soon enough. It so happened that on the way home, she once again bought a Mango-Banana Mush-a-Slush.

And whom did she run into in the market? None other than Judge Merkin, dressed in his fine suit and coat.

"So, Your Honor," Cricket said, approaching the judge. "You have ruled that my entire day is worth only a single dollar."

"Why yes," said the amused judge, recognizing the young woman. "And a splendid ruling it was."

"In that case, here," Cricket said.

And she proceeded to pour her Mush-a-Slush over the judge's head. "Now *your* day is ruined! You can collect your dollar from Mr. Blunt when he brings it to your courtroom tomorrow."

**THE END**

---

( Model )

Cricket was 2 hours and 40 minutes late to work. She was supposed to show up at 8:45 A.M. At what time did she get to work?

Step 1:

```
   8 hr 45 min    [8:45 A.M.]
+  2 hr 40 min    [late]
  ─────────────
  10 hr 25 min  →  10 hr + 1 hr 25 min
```

Step 2:

```
  10 hr
+  1 hr 25 min
  ─────────────
  11 hr 25 min  →  11:25 A.M.
```

---

**Find the sums and differences.**

13. 3 hr 5 min + 4 hr 43 min = _____

14. 1 hr 36 min + 2 hr 51 min = _____

15. 6:10 P.M. + 3 hr 32 min = _____

16. 4 hr 35 min – 1 hr 28 min = _____

17. 10:15 A.M. – 2 hr 30 min = _____

18. 9 hr 12 min – 8 hr 55 min = _____

Name _____ Date _____

## Giraffe and Bear Have Dinner

At the watering hole, a Giraffe and a Bear struck up a friendship. They both liked philosophy and music. They talked endlessly about the nature of goodness, and other such lofty things.

Finally, Giraffe said, "I must invite you to dinner, old chum."

"That would be marvelous!" cried Bear.

A date was set, and Bear arrived at the Giraffe's house right on time. They talked for a bit about the nature of goodness, then it was time to eat.

"I have a special treat for us tonight," said Bear. "See those tree-tops over there? I've saved them for our dinner. They contain some of the sweetest green leaves you'll ever eat."

"Tree-tops, eh?" said Bear. "That sounds splendid!"

And it was splendid—for Giraffe, anyway. He went munching away at the leaves on the high tree tops while Bear stood forlornly below, unable to get even close to the top branches. When the leaves were finally gone, Giraffe, who had been so busy eating that he barely noticed Bear below, said:

"Wasn't that delicious, good friend?"

"Oh yes," replied Bear politely. "Next week you *must* come to my house and have dinner with me."

So the date was set, and the following week Giraffe arrived at Bear's.

"I too have a special treat for us," said Bear. "These low bushes in the gully have some of the juiciest berries you'll ever find. Come, good friend, let's enjoy."

So Bear proceeded to gobble up the berries while Giraffe tried—without any luck—to bend over low enough to reach even one of them. The gully was just too low and irregular, and the Giraffe's neck and legs were too long, so he got nothing for dinner.

When the berries were all gone, Bear said, "Well, friend, I hope you have enjoyed my hospitality."

"Oh indeed," said Giraffe graciously. "We must do this again very soon."

"I agree," said Bear. "As soon as possible."

So Giraffe went home. And though they both shared many interests, neither one of them ever invited the other to dinner again.

**THE END**

**Name** _____ **Date** _____

---

( Model )

Walking slowly, it took Bear 23 minutes to travel the 713 yards to Giraffe's house. What was Bear's rate of speed? At this rate, how long would it take Bear to go 930 yards to the forest?

This is a multistep problem. First, divide 713 yards by 23 minutes to find out Bear's rate of speed.

$713 \div 23 = 31$ yards per minute

Next, to find out how long it would take Bear to travel 930 yards, divide the distance by his rate of speed, so:

$930 \div 31 = 30$ minutes

---

1. Giraffe ate 224 leaves in 7 minutes. How many leaves did he eat each minute? At this rate, how many leaves could Giraffe eat in 12 minutes?

_____

2. Both Bear and Giraffe are fast readers. It took Bear 17 hours to read a 442-page book. Giraffe finished a 341-page book in 11 hours. Who is the faster reader? By how many pages per hour?

_____

3. Bear ate berries at a rate of 15 berries per minute for 24 minutes. How many berries did she eat in all?

_____

4. Bear got a job picking berries. She picked 61 berries a minute for 35 minutes. Unfortunately, she ate 12 berries per minute while she was picking. How many berries did Bear pick in all?

_____

5. Giraffe got a job picking leaves that paid $202.50 for 30 hours of work. Bear's job paid $6.60 per hour. Who was paid at a higher rate— Giraffe or Bear? By how much?

_____

6. Bear worked for 8.5 hours at a rate of $6.60 per hour. Then she worked 3.5 hours overtime at a rate of $9.90 per hour. How much did Bear make in all? What was Bear's average rate of pay for the entire day?

_____

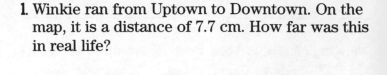 

**Name** _____  **Date** _____

## The Baa Baa Police Report
### Reported by Baa Baa Black Sheep

Fairy Land—I'm Baa Baa Black Sheep, and this is the Baa Baa Police Report. Today, we'll focus on well-known jewel thief Wee Willie Winkie. Recently, Winkie was seen *"running through the town, upstairs and downstairs, in his nightgown!"*

In his *nightgown*! Was this Winkie planning some kind of heist? Witnesses report this fellow to be *"rapping at the windows, prying through the lock."* So now Baa Baa must ask:

*"Are all the children safe in bed?"* For now it's eight o'clock.

---( Model )---

**Wee Willie Winkie ran from Uptown to Midtown. This distance measured 3.3 centimeters on the map. How far did Winkie run?**

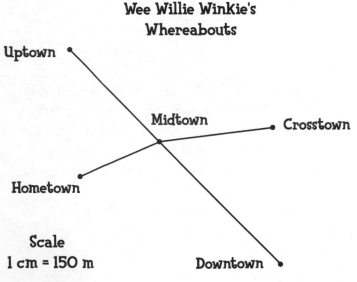

Wee Willie Winkie's
Whereabouts

Uptown
Midtown • Crosstown
Hometown
Scale
1 cm = 150 m      Downtown

3.3 cm x 150 = 495 meters

1. Winkie ran from Uptown to Downtown. On the map, it is a distance of 7.7 cm. How far was this in real life?

_____

2. The map distance from Crosstown through Midtown to Downtown is 7.3 cm. How far is this in real distance?

_____

3. Winkie ran a distance of 345 meters from Midtown to Hometown. On the map, what distance does this represent?

_____

4. Off the main road, the distance from Crosstown to Downtown is 3.4 cm on the map. How far does this represent in meters?

_____

5. Winkie ran a total of 2700 meters in all. How many centimeters would this be on the map?

_____

Name _____   Date _____

Our second situation focuses on an equally familiar figure—crime boss Little Jack Horner. Oh, Horner's the tricky one! Here's what he *says* happened: He, Little Jack Horner, *sat in a corner, eating a mincemeat pie.* Here's how eye-witnesses describe what happened next: "Horner *stuck in his thumb*—and then, what does he do? He *pulls out a plum!* Imagine. Then he says, '*What a good boy am I!*'"

A good boy, indeed!

Again, Baa Baa has only one question: *What is a whole PLUM doing in the middle of a pie?*

"I have no idea," says Detective Mary Mary Quite Contrary. "Perhaps it was planted there to cover up Horner's criminal activities."

Cover up, indeed!

Our third incident involves none other than Little Miss Muffet herself! That's right, she's back. And she's still sitting on that *tuffet*, and she's still eating her *curds and whey.*

Here again is where the story gets interesting, as reporter Little Boy Blue describes: "*Along came a spider, who sat down beside her.*" And you'll never guess what happened next.

*It frightened Miss Muffet away!*

Could the spider have been hired by Horner or Winkie to frighten Muffet away from their crime turf? When questioned, the spider denied involvement with the two notorious characters.

At this point, all Baa Baa can say is stay tuned, folks, as more information becomes available. With that, this is Baa Baa Black Sheep signing off with the question, *Do I have any wool?* with the same answer as always:

*Yes sir, yes sir, three bags full!*

### THE END

Solve the problems using Baa Baa's Metro Crime Map, which has a scale of 1 inch equaling 2.5 miles.

6. Reporter Little Boy Blue drove 8 miles to get to a crime scene. How many inches does this represent on the Metro Crime Map?

_____

7. Detective Contrary measured out 9 inches on the Metro Crime Map. How far is this in miles?

_____

8. Little Boy Blue knows that the distance from the sheep's meadow to the cows in the corn is 5 miles. How many inches is this on the map?

_____

Name _____  Date _____

## The Hoop in the Stone

A long time ago, in the early days of hoop-playing, there was a Stone Hoop that stood ten feet above a rock in a lake. Legend said: *Whosoever dunketh inneth this hoop—that person shall be king*! Translation: Dunk and you rule!

The trouble was, in those days no one knew what "dunk" meant. They thought "dunk" was something you did with a donut and coffee, so the whole thing made little sense.

In fact, in those days they played with a *square* ball. Actually the ball was cube-shaped, with square faces. They called it the "cube."

You can imagine all the trouble this cube caused. Handling the cube was tricky. Passing was inconsistent. Dribbling was nearly impossible because you never knew how and where this cube might bounce next.

Along came a youth named Arthur with a new invention for the game.

"I call my invention the *ball*," Arthur said.

Arthur presented his ball to the famous Knights of the Square Table, on the shores of the lake, near the famed Stone Hoop.

Arthur dribbled, passed, and made shots. The knights were not impressed.

"This *ball* is the work of an evil spirit," said one.

"What's wrong with our old cube?" asked another.

"Surely, this *ball* will put an end to our beloved game," said a third.

At the end of his demonstration, Arthur was angry. If they couldn't see that *his* ball was better, he would show them. So he grabbed the ball. And he approached the famed Stone Hoop.

Slowly, Arthur went into his wind-up. He dribbled down the lane with his ball. Then he rose majestically, the lake in the background, the ball in his right hand—soaring higher and higher—until he came down and sunk it in the hoop with a thundering smash.

The dunk was born!

( Model )

**What is the circumference of (distance around) this circular stone hoop with a 9-inch radius?**

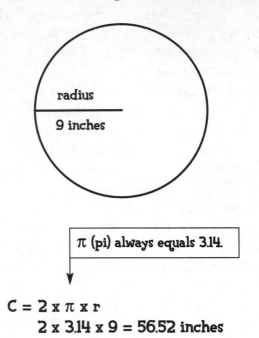

radius
9 inches

π (pi) always equals 3.14.

$$C = 2 \times \pi \times r$$
$$2 \times 3.14 \times 9 = 56.52 \text{ inches}$$

1. Find the circumference of a hoop with a radius of 7 inches.

_____

2. Find the circumference of a hoop with a radius of 20 cm.

_____

3. Find the circumference of a hoop with a radius of 35 inches.

_____

Name _____  Date _____

**4.** Find the circumference of a circle with a radius of 100 yards.

_____

**5.** Find the circumference of a circle with a radius of 10 feet.

_____

And the council was impressed. Suddenly, for the first time ever, everyone began to understand the legend: *Whosoever dunketh . . . that person shall be king!*

And soon Arthur was king—of the basketball courts, that is. A single dunk had changed everything. Suddenly basketball—as the game was now known—was all the rage. All the kids were playing it and clamoring for this new ball.

Arthur, or *King* Arthur as he was now known, joined the league and became a legendary player and a true master of the ball. As a result of Arthur's ball, everything improved. Dribbling got better. Passing got better. Shooting got better.

And it remains that way today.

### THE END

**Epilogue**
The Knights of the Square Table, in keeping with the trend of things, changed their name to The Knights of the Round Table.

_____( Model )_____

**What is the area of a hoop with a 6-inch radius?**

Area = π x r² =
3.14 x 6 x 6 = 113.04 sq in

_____

**6.** The Round Table has a circular shape and an 8-foot radius. What is its area?

8 ft

Area = _____

**7.** Find the area of this circle.

12 m

Area = _____

**8.** Find the circumference and the area of this circle.

9.5 cm

Area = _____

Circumference = _____

**9.** Find the area of the shaded region.
(Hint: Subtract the area of the small circle from the area of the large circle.)

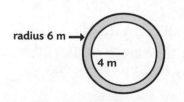

radius 6 m →

4 m

Area = _____

Name _____     Date _____

## The Leopard in the Cage

Lion, Mouse, and Rabbit all liked to tell stories, but sometimes they disagreed about a story's moral. They all disagreed about the moral to a story called the Leopard in the Cage.

*A leopard got caught in a cage. The animals celebrated, but then saw that the cage door was not fully locked. A volunteer needed to flip the latch to keep the leopard locked in. Who would do it? No one spoke up, until finally tiny Mouse said, "I will!" The other animals laughed. But in the end, Mouse got the job done and the animals were saved.*

When they finished with this story, Rabbit asked, "What's the moral?"

"First, I'd like to say: wasn't that a great story?" Mouse said.

"I don't think it was so great," Rabbit said. "I like stories with rabbits in them."

"Well, I *liked* this story," Mouse said. "And here is the moral: *Mice have more courage than other animals.*"

"That's a ridiculous moral!" said Rabbit.

"Why?" said Mouse. "The mouse volunteered to flip the latch. The mouse had more courage. It's as simple as that."

( Model )

Here is the latch in three different positions. Study the chart below. Which position shows an obtuse angle? A right angle? An acute angle? A straight angle?

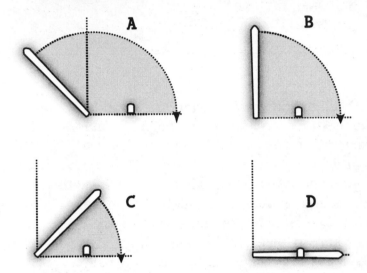

Angle A is obtuse. Angle B is a right angle. Angle C is acute. Angle D is a straight angle.

Identify each angle as acute, obtuse, right, or straight.

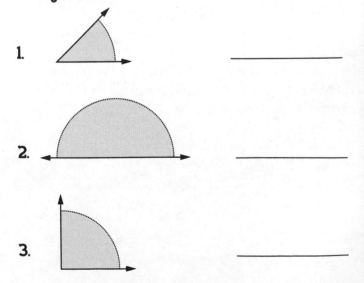

1. _____

2. _____

3. _____

Name _____  Date _____

**4.**  _____

Identify the angles in each shape as acute, obtuse, or a right angle. Use a letter to identify each angle. If an angle is not represented in a particular figure, write "None."

**5.**  _____

**6.** 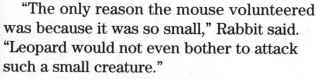 _____

**7.** parallelogram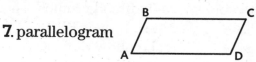

acute: _____  obtuse: _____  right: _____

"The only reason the mouse volunteered was because it was so small," Rabbit said. "Leopard would not even bother to attack such a small creature."

"That's not true," Mouse said.

"Yes, it is," said Rabbit.

Here, Rabbit and Mouse began to argue. They kept getting louder and louder, until finally Lion cleared his throat.

Both animals looked at Lion. "What about you, Mr. Lion?" they said. "What do you see as the moral?"

"Hmm, that's a tough one," Lion said. "How about, *Compared to a lion, a leopard is a coward and fool.*"

"Now THAT is truly ridiculous," Rabbit said. "Lion's moral has nothing to do with the story."

"So what? It's still true," Lion said.

Here, Mouse and Rabbit once again started arguing. They might have come to blows had not Lion suddenly stood.

"Here's a moral that perhaps both of you can understand," he said. "*A lion could eat everyone here if he felt like it.*"

For a moment, all three of them fell silent. Then Rabbit finally spoke up.

"Hmm," said Rabbit. "That's not bad. I like it."

"I agree," said Mouse. "Lion's moral has a lot of truth to it."

So they all agreed that Lion's moral was best. Even though it had nothing to do with the story itself.

**THE END**

**8.** triangle

acute: _____  obtuse: _____  right: _____

**9.** trapezoid

acute: _____  obtuse: _____  right: _____

**10.** rectangle

acute: _____  obtuse: _____  right: _____

**11.** triangle

acute: _____  obtuse: _____  right: _____

**12.** hexagon

acute: _____  obtuse: _____  right: _____

**Name** _____ **Date** _____

## Hansel and Gretel, Lost on the Internet

Hansel and Gretel lived in a small house with their father, who had an Internet business.

The Web site sold specialty bread crumbs. The crumbs came in four varieties: Honey, PB&J, Cranberry Raisin, and Marshmallow-Surprise.

The only trouble was—who wanted specialty bread crumbs? Hardly anyone! Needless to say, the children's father's business was not doing too well.

So one day the children's father said to Hansel and Gretel: "I want you to go on the Internet and look for customers." Then he added, "Remember, if you ever get lost, you can always "go back" to our home page."

The children logged on to the Internet and one link led to another. Before long they found themselves deep in the World Wide Web on a dark and spooky Web site.

"Where are we?" asked Hansel nervously.

"I'm n-not sure," stammered Gretel.

――――――――――( Model )――――――――――

A single Web site links to 2 new sites. Each of those new sites links to 2 sites, and, finally, those sites also link to 2 sites each. How many sites are there in all?

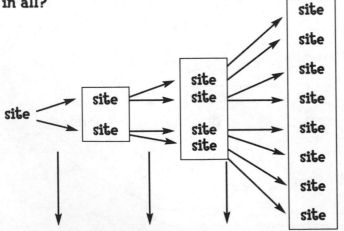

2 links x 2 links x 2 links = $2^3$ = 8 sites

### Write in standard form.

1. $2^2$ _____

2. $2^4$ _____

3. $3^2$ _____

4. $2^5$ _____

5. $3^3$ _____

6. $4^2$ _____

7. $4^3$ _____

8. $3^5$ _____

### Write in exponent form.

9. 4 x 4 x 4 _____

10. 2 x 2 x 2 x 2 _____

11. 5 x 5 x 5 _____

12. 6 x 6 x 6 x 6 x 6 _____

13. 8 x 8 x 8 x 8 x 8 x 8 _____

14. 10 x 10 x 10 _____

Name _____ Date _____

Soon Hansel and Gretel came to a chat room full of potential customers who were discussing bread crumbs.

"Father will love this!" cried Hansel.

"If only he could be here!" cried Gretel.

The chat room was perfect! They wanted to get home to tell him about it but when they tried to link out of it, the virtual face of a kindly lady appeared on the screen and said: ACCESS DENIED! Hansel began to worry that they might never get back to their home page again.

"Don't be silly," Gretel told him. "We can always just reboot the machine." But when they pressed RESTART the virtual face of the kindly lady suddenly turned into a hideous virtual witch!

"You are bad children," the witch announced. "And you will never get back to your home page because I am going to destroy it! Ha ha ha ha ha ha ha!" the witch cackled.

"Oh no!" Hansel cried. "Without a home page, Father's business will be lost! What will we do?"

"Don't worry," said Gretel. "I have an idea."

"Is it a magic spell?" asked Hansel.

"No," said Gretel. "It's more powerful than that."

"Is it a shining knight on a white horse?" asked Hansel.

"No," said Gretel. "It's more powerful than that, too."

"Then what is it?" Hansel asked.

Indeed, what could be more powerful than a magic spell or even a heroic knight on a shining white horse?

"It's CONTROL-ALT-DELETE," Gretel said.

Before Hansel could even ask what CONTROL-ALT-DELETE was, Gretel had already pushed the buttons that could shut down any computer program. And shut down they did. Within seconds, the evil virtual witch went away. The ACCESS DENIED messages went away.

"Phew!" said Hansel and Gretel.

They restarted the computer, went back to their home page, and from then on, things turned out wonderfully. Their computer wasn't damaged. Their father's business wasn't destroyed.

In fact, his site even started to do a booming business! They would soon be rich!

And if you think a person can get rich selling *bread crumbs*, then you *really* believe in fairy tales!

### THE END

Write >, <, or = in the box.

15. $3^3$ _____ $2^5$

16. $4^2$ _____ $2^4$

17. $3^4$ _____ $4^3$

18. $5^3$ _____ $12^2$

19. $6^3$ _____ $4^4$

20. $5^4$ _____ $4^5$

Name _____ Date _____

## The Grand Fool Fest

Queen Mona the Wise loved foolishness, so she invited dozens of fools to her kingdom for a Grand Fool Fest. For days the fools competed against one another in a Grand Fool-Off. They stumbled and bumbled, they sang silly songs and they made stupid faces. All competed to see who could become the Grand Fool and receive a special prize.

───────( Model )───────

In the Stumbling event, Abner the Addled (A) finished ahead of Biddie the Bewildered (B), but behind Curva the Confused (C). Darvin the Dense (D) was beaten out by Curva and Abner. In what order did the four fools finish?

Use letters A, B, C, and D for the four fools.

Fact: A > B          Order: A then B
Fact: A < C          Order: C then A then B
Fact: D < C & A      Order: C then A then D then B

1. In the Bumbling event, J finished behind K, but ahead of L. M was beaten out by J but not L. In what order did the four finish?

_____

_____

2. In the Silly Song event, P finished behind Q and R, but ahead of S. Q did not finish first. In what order did the four finish?

_____

_____

3. In the Nonsense event, A scored better than B and C. C was ahead of B but behind D, who just beat out A. In what order did the fools finish?

_____

_____

After a tough competition, three finalists competed to see who could be the Grand Fool.

The first finalist was Leopold the Lout. All eyes focused on Leopold as he took out a clean toothbrush and proceeded to brush his teeth with hot tar.

"Ooo-o-o-h!" groaned the onlookers. "That's some nasty toothpaste. What a lout!"

Not to be outdone, the next contestant, Knucklehead Nora combed her hair with pure honey. At first, this just seemed only mildly foolish—until the bees started to arrive. And it wasn't long before Nora was being chased out the door by a pair of hungry brown bears!

"What a true knucklehead!" cried the onlookers, eager to see the third and final contestant.

**Name** _____ **Date** _____

He was named Durf. All Durf did was put his pants on upside down and backwards over his head. It was a surprisingly simple, yet very stupid act.

The audience roared with delight.

"This oaf must have cheese for brains!" quipped one onlooker.

Now it was time to pass out the awards.

"You were all so splendidly foolish," gushed Queen Mona, "that I still can't choose between you. So I've decided to give you each a prize."

She handed a silver chalice to Leopold the Lout. Knucklehead Nora received a ruby ring. And Durf?

"To you, Durf, I give an award of nothing," Queen Mona said. "Because you strike me as such a numbskull that I feel that any award I give would just be wasted."

"What if I refuse to accept your award?" said Durf.

"Then I will toss you in the dungeon," said the Queen.

And so it was done. Durf refused.

The Queen threw him in the dungeon.

The Queen had found her Grand Fool. And Durf was such an utter fool that he was happy about the whole thing.

**THE END**

4. On the Forest Road, Durf traveled from the Castle to towns A, B, C, and D. B was closer to the Castle than A. C was between A and B. D was between A and C. In what order did the towns appear?

_____

_____

5. The towns of E, F, G, and H were on the River Road. G was farther from the Castle than F, but closer than E. H was farther than E. In what order did the towns appear?

_____

_____

6. Durf put on his boots before his socks. He put on his shirt before he put on his boots and after he put on his coat. In what order did Durf dress?

_____

_____

Name _____    Date _____

## The Prince and the Bakery Boy

Young Prince Roy was walking past a bake shop when he spied a boy about his age. The two stood side by side.

"You look *just* like me!" Prince Roy cried. It was true. The prince and the bakery boy were *exact* doubles of one another.

"I've got an idea," whispered the prince. "Let's switch places. You become a prince. I'll become a bakery boy."

"Why would you want to do that?" said the bakery boy. "You have everything. I have nothing."

"But you are free," said Prince Roy. "I am forever told where to go and what to do. I want to see what it's like to be free."

"Very well," said the bakery boy. So the two traded places. In a month's time, they agreed to meet at the castle and switch back to their old identities.

---

( Model )

Prince Roy has 3 pounds (48 ounces) of dough. Without any waste, how many ways can he make bread if he includes at least one 30-ounce loaf?

> **BREAD MENU**
>
> 3-ounce Rolls
> 14-ounce Small Loaf
> 30-ounce Large Loaf

Make a table. The total doesn't add to 48, so try again.

| 30 x 1 | 14 x 1 | 3 x 1 | Total |
|--------|--------|-------|-------|
| 30     | 14     | 3     | 47    |

| 30 x 1 | 14 x 0 | 3 x 6 | Total |
|--------|--------|-------|-------|
| 30     | 0      | 18    | 48    |

**This combination works.**

---

1. How can Prince Roy make only one type of bread and use up all 48 ounces of his dough?

   _____

   _____

2. How can Prince Roy make bread using at least 1 small loaf?

   _____

Name _____ Date _____

Over the month the bakery boy learned what it was like to be a prince. To have servants. To eat grand food and wear fine clothing. To be taught by the Royal Tutors and ride horses from the Royal Stables.

Meanwhile Prince Roy learned what it was like to be free to do such things as work in the bakery all day long, haul flour, chop firewood, and scrub floors. He also learned what it was like to live in a small village among common people. It was a tough life, but it was free.

When the month was up, Prince Roy came to the castle.

"What a great experience," he told the bakery boy. "I have learned so much about freedom. I have learned that freedom is a good thing, but freedom is not everything. What have you learned, my friend?"

The bakery boy, dressed in his fine princely clothing, frowned.

"Who are you?" he asked.

"Why, don't be silly," said Prince Roy. "I am the prince. You are my double. We agreed to meet here in one month's time so we could switch places."

A curious smile came over the bakery boy's face.

"Ah yes," he said. "We did agree to meet in one month's time. But not to switch places. Why would I want to switch places with a bakery boy?"

Prince Roy protested here, but who would believe a bakery boy over a prince?

As he was being carried away by the guards, Prince Roy had to admit, the bakery boy had learned quite a bit in his short time as "prince." Quite a bit indeed.

**THE END**

**Suppose Prince Roy has 64 ounces of dough.**

3. If he bakes at least one 30-ounce loaf, how can he finish the job without any waste?

_____

_____

4. What other way can the prince finish the job without any waste?

_____

_____

**Suppose Prince Roy now has 96 ounces of dough. How can he finish the job using:**

5. At least two 30-ounce loaves?

_____

_____

6. One 30-ounce loaf and at least one 14-ounce loaf?

_____

_____

Name _____ Date _____

## Uncle Goose

You've heard of Mother Goose, but how about Uncle Goose—her brother-in-law? While Mother Goose is famous for her rhymes and songs, Uncle Goose is not so well known. Even so, many experts think that Uncle Goose's stories are almost as good as Mother Goose's—except for one thing: Uncle Goose's stories are a little off-key; a little weird.

In fact, some of Uncle Goose's stories are *very* weird. To see what we mean, take a look at this famous Mother Goose rhyme:

**Jack Sprat could eat no fat, his wife could eat no lean. And so between the two of them, they picked the platter clean.**

Now take a look at Uncle Goose's version of the story:

**Joe Sproe could eat no dough, his wife no tomatoes or cheese. So instead of pizza take-out, they always got Chinese.**

A little weird, eh? Convinced yet? Here's another from Mother Goose:

**Sing a song of sixpence, a pocket full of rye, Four and twenty blackbirds baked in a pie: When the pie was opened, the birds began to sing; And wasn't that a dainty dish to set before the king?**

**The king was in the parlour, counting out his money; The queen was in the kitchen, eating bread and honey; The maid was in the garden, hanging out the clothes, Along came a blackbird and snapped off her nose!**

And now, the Uncle Goose version:

**Sing a song of Internet, red, blue, and green, Four and twenty pop-ups on my computer screen. When the site was opened, pop-ups began to flash; What a crazy Web site, I hope this doesn't crash!**

**My dad was at the fax machine, trying to fix a jam; My mom was in the office, reading e-mail spam; My sister was on her home page, working out some bugs, Along came baby brother, and yanked out the plug!**

And finally, another familiar one from Mother Goose:

**Little Boy Blue, come, blow your horn! The sheep's in the meadow, the cow's in the corn. Where's the little boy that looks after the sheep? Under the haystack, fast asleep!**

And from Uncle Goose:

**Little Boy Green, come, blow your top! You're late to work, your car's in the shop. Where is the taxi, who said he'd come fast? He's back at the gas station, out of gas!**

**THE END**

Name _____    Date _____

---

### Model

Two different Web sites show pop-up ads every 6 minutes and 8 minutes. If both sites are now displaying pop-up ads, how long will it take before they are both showing an ad at the same time again?

Find the Least Common Multiple, or LCM:

Multiples of 6: 6, 12, 18, (24), 30

Multiples of 8: 8, 16, (24), 32    LCM = 24

---

### Find the LCM.

1. 4 and 6 _____

2. 5 and 10 _____

3. 3 and 5 _____

4. 6 and 3 _____

5. 6 and 9 _____

6. 8 and 10 _____

7. 12 and 9 _____

8. 15 and 9 _____

---

### Model

Find the Greatest Common Factor, or GCF, of 12 and 18.

Factors of 12: (3 x 2) x 2

Factors of 18: 3 x (3 x 2)    GCF = 6

---

### Find the GCF.

9. 10 and 15 _____

10. 8 and 10 _____

11. 9 and 12 _____

12. 12 and 20 _____

13. 16 and 24 _____

14. 15 and 45 _____

15. 30 and 42 _____

16. 48 and 72 _____

# Answer Key

**pages 8–9**
1. 40; 0
2. 20; 0
3. 120; 100
4. 280; 300
5. 2140; 2100
6. 2,000; 0
7. 5,000; 0
8. 19,000; 20,000
9. 32,000; 30,000
10. 50,000; 50,000
11. 453,000; 450,000
12. 47,000
13. 140
14. They got the same.
15. Neither; Simpson the Stooge

**pages 10–11**
1. 60
2. 70
3. 30
4. 30
5. 800
6. 100
7. 40
8. 700
9. 1200
10. 400
11. 90
12. 500
13. 900
14. 3500
15. 4800
16. about 130 different things
17. Yes, because 8 x 50 = 400 and he had more than 50 ounces.

**page 13**
1. b
2. a
3. b
4. a, d
5. b, c
6. 468
7. true
8. false, 35 is not divisible by 3
9. true

**pages 14–15**
1. commutative property of addition
2. zero property
3. identity property of addition
4. identity property of multiplication
5. commutative property of multiplication
6. 1, identity property of multiplication
7. 5 + 4, commutative property of addition
8. 0, identity property of addition
9. 2, 3, commutative property of multiplication
10. 0, zero property
11. associative property of multiplication
12. distributive property
13. associative property of addition
14. 5, 7, distributive property
15. 2 + 7, associative property of addition
16. 7, 5 associative property of multiplication

**page 17**
1. 10 feet
2. 92 feet
3. 2 inches
4. 2 feet
5. 1 foot
6. inches
7. feet
8. feet
9. feet
10. inches
11. feet
12. inches
13. feet
14. inches

**page 19**
1. 36
2. 18
3. 76
4. 4
5. 7
6. 3
7. 113
8. 20
9. 180
10. 42 ft 504 in
11. 54 in
12. 285 yd
13. 10,260 in

**page 21**
1. f
2. c
3. a
4. e
5. b
6. d
7. f
8. c

**pages 22–23**
1. quadrilateral
2. triangle
3. hexagon
4. quadrilateral
5. triangle
6. quadrilateral
7. It is 4-sided.
8. Yes, opposite sides are parallel, and at least two sides are congruent.
9. No, all angles are equal and sides are equal.
10. Yes, all angles are equal.
11. Yes, there are 4 congruent sides.
12. Yes, there are equal sides and equal angles.
13. A square is a quadrilateral with opposite sides parallel, 4 right angles, and all sides congruent.

**pages 24–25**
1. 20 + 10 + 10 + 50 +10
2. 20 + 20 + 5 + 50 + 5
3. 50 + 20 + 10 + 10 + 5 + 5
4. 50 + 10 +10 +10 +10 +10
5. 5, 15
6. 6, 21
7. There is always one more than the last time.

**pages 26–27**
1. 5:4, 5/4, 1.25
2. 3:10, 3/10, 0.3
3. 2:5, 2/5, 0.4
4. 9:3, 15:5
5. 6/9, 2/3
6. 6:1
7. 8:5
8. 3:2
9. 3:2, 2:3

**page 29**
1. 15/6, 2.5 to 1
2. 9/4, 2 1/4 to 1
3. 12 feet
4. 75 meters
5. 49 inches
6. 5.6 inches
7. 22.5 inches
8. 6.4 feet
9. 500 feet

**page 31**
1. 1064 to 1069
2. 1067
3. 15
4. 1065
5. between 1065 and 1066
6. 1064, 1068
7. 1066, 1069
8. 1066–1067

**page 33**
1. 95
2. chicken
3. pig
4. 5
5. 245
6. 38.8%
7. fish and pigs
8. about 2/7

**pages 34–35**
1. 33
2. 100
3. 33/100
4. 33%
5. 1/4
6. ocean and portrait
7. pizza
8. 200
9. 2/5
10. 4/5
11. apple/banana and peanut butter sandwich

**pages 36–37**
1. 14
2. 14
3. 14
4. 8.27
5. 2
6. Change: -6.27
7. 8 and 2; Change: -6
8. 8 and 0; Change: -8

**pages 38–39**
1. P(dream or tug) = 2/5
2. P(little weird) = 1/5
3. P(weird) = 2/5
4. 3/5
5. 4/5
6. 0/5
7. 1/10
8. P = 2/5 x 1/2= 2/10 = 1/5
9. P = 3/5 x 1/2= 3/10

**pages 40–41**
1. 1 hr 40 min
2. 97 min
3. 185 min
4. 7 hr 11 min
5. 1 d 2 hr
6. 55 hr
7. 157 hr
8. 25 d
9. 14 wk 2 d
10. 1 yr 23 wk
11. 3020 d
12. 2 yr 270 d
13. 7 hr 48 min
14. 4 hr 27 min
15. 9:42 P.M.
16. 3 hr 7 min
17. 7:45 A.M.
18. 17 min

**page 43**
1. 32; 384
2. Bear: 26 pages per hour; Giraffe: 31 pages per hour; Bear is faster by 5 pages per hour
3. 360
4. 1715 berries
5. Giraffe: $6.75 per hour, Bear: $6.60 per hour; Giraffe by $0.15 an hour
6. $90.75, $7.56/hr average

**pages 44–45**
1. 1155 m
2. 1095 m
3. 2.3 cm
4. 510 m
5. 18
6. 3.2 in
7. 22.5 mi
8. 2 in

**pages 46–47**
1. 43.96 in
2. 125.6 cm
3. 219.8 in
4. 628 yd
5. 62.8 ft
6. 200.96 sq ft
7. 452.16 sq m
8. circumference = 59.66 cm, area = 283.385 sq cm
9. 62.8 sq m

**pages 48–49**
1. acute
2. straight
3. right
4. acute
5. obtuse
6. acute
7. acute: a and c; obtuse: b and d; right: none

8. acute: e and g; obtuse: f; right: none
9. acute: i and j; obtuse: h and k; right: none
10. acute: none; obtuse: none; right: l, m, n, and o
11. acute: q and r; obtuse: none; right: p
12. acute: s and v; obtuse: t, u, x, and w; right: none

**pages 50–51**
1. 4
2. 16
3. 9
4. 32
5. 27
6. 16
7. 64
8. 243
9. $4^3$
10. $2^4$
11. $5^3$
12. $6^5$
13. $8^6$
14. $10^3$
15. <
16. =
17. >
18. <
19. <
20. <

**pages 52–53**
1. KJML
2. RQPS
3. DACB
4. BCDA
5. FGEH
6. coat, shirt, boots, socks

**pages 54–55**
1. 16 three-ounce rolls
2. 3 small 14-ounce loafs, two 3-ounce rolls
3. one 30-ounce loaf, two 14-ounce loaves, two 3-ounce loaves
4. two 14-ounce loaves, twelve 3-ounce loaves
5. 2 ways: three 30-ounce loaves, two 3-ounce loaves; and two 30-ounce loaves, twelve 3-ounce loaves
6. 1 way: one 30-ounce loaf, three 14-ounce loaves, eight 3-ounce loaves

**pages 56–57**
1. 12
2. 10
3. 15
4. 6
5. 18
6. 40
7. 36
8. 45
9. 5
10. 2
11. 3
12. 4
13. 8
14. 15
15. 6
16. 24

 Notes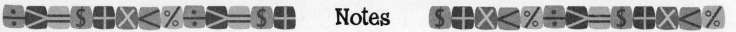

 **Notes**

 Notes

 Notes